PRAYERS ON WHEELS

Michael Kwatera, OSB

Resource Publications, Inc.
San Jose, California

Reprint Department
Resource Publications, Inc.
160 E. Virginia St. #290
San Jose, CA 95112-5876
(408) 286-8505
(408) 287-8748 fax

Library of Congress Cataloging-in-Publication Data

Kwatera, Michael.
Prayers on wheels / Michael Kwatera.
p. cm.
ISBN 0-89390-605-0
1. Family--Prayer-books and devotions--English. 2. Catholic Church--Prayer-books and devotions--English. 3. Automobile travel--Prayer-books and devotions--English. I. Title.

BX2170.F3K93 2004
242'.8--dc22

2004046778

Printed in the United States
04 05 06 07 08 | 5 4 3 2 1

Production Staff: Nelson Estarija, Elizabeth Gebelein, Susan Carter

ACKNOWLEDGMENTS

The English translation of the psalms and a select number of refrains for the psalms from the *Contemporary English Version* © American Bible Society 1991, 1995. Used by permission.

Scripture quotations (other than for the psalms) are from *Good News Bible with Deutero-Canonicals/Apocrypha: The Bible in Today's English* Version © American Bible Society 1966, 1971, 1976, 1979. Used by permission.

Prayers no. 1, 3, 4, and 5 in the section entitled "Various Travel Prayers" are based in part on texts included in *Catholic Household Blessings & Prayers* (Washington, D.C.: United States Catholic Conference, Inc., 1988).

Dedicated to my aunt,
Sister Mary Rose Stecz, OSF (1910–2002),
with thanks for teaching me much about good writing
and even more about constant praying.

CONTENTS

Introduction 1

Prayers for Occasions and Activities

Heading Off to School and Returning

1. First Day of Classes 4
2. Going to School 4
3. Before Taking Tests 5
4. Returning from School 5
5. Going to a Religious Education Class 6
6. Taking a Child to Boarding School or College 6
7. Visiting a Child at a Boarding School or College 7
8. Going to Graduation Exercises or Party 7

Doing Things

9. Bringing a Newborn Infant Home from the Hospital 8
10. Eating a Meal in the Car 8
11. Going on an Adventure 9
12. Going Fishing 9
13. Going Hunting 10
14. Going to Practice 10
15. Going to a Game, Meet, or Tournament 11
16. Going Shopping 12
17. Going on a Sleep-over 12
18. Going to Sunday Eucharist or Sunday Worship 13
19. Going Trick-or-Treating on Halloween 13
20. Going on Vacation 14
21. Going to Work 14
22. Learning to Drive a Car 15
23. Stopping to Marvel at God's Creation 15
24. Taking a Child to a Date 16
25. Visiting Friends 16

Going Places

26. Going to an Amusement Park 17
27. Going to a Birthday Party 17
28. Going to the Cabin. 18
29. Returning from the Cabin 18
30. Going to a Concert or Recital 18
31. Going to the Doctor or Dentist 19
32. Going to the Emergency Room 19
33. Going to the Movies 20
34. Going to a Play 20
35. Going out to Eat 21
36. Going to a Picnic or Barbeque 21
37. Going to Summer Camp 22
38. Going to the Zoo or Animal Park. 22
39. Taking a Sick or Injured Pet to the Veterinarian
or Animal Hospital 23

Visiting Family Members

40. Going to a Family Gathering or Reunion. 24
41. Taking a Child to Visit a Divorced Parent 24
42. Visiting a Child or Parent in the Hospital 25
43. Visiting a Sick Relative or Friend at Home 25
44. Visiting Grandparents 26

Celebrating Special Religious Occasions

45. Baptism 27
46. First Holy Communion or Confirmation 27
47. Wake or Funeral 28
48. Wedding 28
49. Wedding Anniversary 29
50. Ordination 29

Facing Trouble on the Road

51. Car Trouble 30
52. During a Storm. 30

53. Looking for a Parking Place 31
54. Stuck in a Traffic Jam 31
55. Waiting at a Stop Light 32
56. Waiting for a Train to Pass 32
57. When Lost 33
58. When Seeing an Ambulance Go By
or Passing the Site of an Accident 33

Prayers for Traveling

Various Travel Prayers 36

Travel Prayer in the Morning 38

Travel Prayer at Noontime 47

Travel Prayer in the Evening 52

Travel Prayer at Night 61

INTRODUCTION

Praying while traveling by car has long been a revered Catholic custom. The rosary was a favorite form of such prayer, and St. Christopher medals have been standard equipment in many Catholic family vehicles. Today's high mobility invites us to explore new prayers to pray on the way.

This booklet originates from the observation by Alice Duffy-Meyer, one of my graduate students, that "we spend a lot of time in the car." I have thought that in our era, family prayer must be prayer around the table, but perhaps the car or minivan is an even more convenient place. Thus, I offer this booklet of prayers for families to use in their goings and comings on wheels.

The prayers at the end of this book are arranged for use at different times of day (morning, noon, evening, and night) while traveling to different places, events, and activities. The format for each time of prayer is kept rather invariable for the sake of familiarity. After an introduction that includes the Sign of the Cross, a psalm asking God's protection is prayed in simple language. Verses are marked for a solo voice, and a short refrain is given for all to pray after each verse. In this way, the driver can take part in praying the psalm.

Several Scripture readings are provided for each time of day, from which the reader can make a selection. Silent reflection on the reading is followed by a short response. Texts of intercessions or prayers of the faithful are not provided, but these may be added, if desired, before the Lord's Prayer. Then a particular closing prayer, apt for the occasion, event, or activity, is prayed by the leader or by all. These prayers, found at the front of the book, can also be prayed singly. Prayers that include the name of a particular person might best be spoken by the leader alone, but on behalf of all. While a number of such prayers are included in this booklet and listed in the table of contents, the wide variety of family activities invites the leader to adapt these prayers or offer a fitting prayer in his or her own words. The prayers provided here can serve as samples. All these prayers end with the same brief conclusion, "We ask this through Christ our Lord," making it easy for all to know when to speak their "Amen." The names that are placed in the blanks, and the gender and number of persons prayed for in these texts, should reflect particular circumstances (for example, if only one grandparent is living). After the closing prayer, words of blessing bring the time of prayer to an end. The ecumenical character of this booklet encourages its use by Christians of all traditions.

The lingering darkness of winter mornings and the early darkness of winter nights may make it difficult or impossible to read the texts from this booklet while sitting in pitch-black darkness. Perhaps over the course of time, some of these texts may find a permanent place in the memory. Night Prayer, especially, has been kept rather lean to make it easy to pray on the way home in the dark. Perhaps a single travel prayer from the collection of prayers in this booklet might be memorized for such occasions.

"When I'm driving, there are certain things I expect from my co-pilot," declares the serious driver in a television commercial. "If you are going to sit in that seat, you've got responsibilities." One of them is to watch the map and to provide navigational information, but another might be to distribute copies of this booklet from the glove compartment and serve as leader of prayer. Other passengers, especially older children, might serve as soloist in the psalm and as reader of the Scripture passage. Once the format becomes familiar, these roles may change voice quite easily.

Michael Kwatera, OSB
July 25, 2004 (formerly the commemoration of St. Christopher, patron of motorists)

PRAYERS FOR OCCASIONS AND ACTIVITIES

HEADING OFF TO SCHOOL AND RETURNING

1. First Day of Classes

Praise to you, God of beginnings,
for bringing us to another school year.
Bless _____ on this first day of classes
as he/she rejoins old friends
and makes new ones.
Make their learning this year
a joy for _____ and for his/her classmates.
Keep their school and playground
free from violence.
We ask this through Christ our Lord. Amen.

2. Going to School

Praise and glory to you,
all-knowing God.
You fill us with questions
about you and about our world.
Send your Holy Spirit
to give light to our minds.
Help _____ to do his/her schoolwork
as well as he/she can.
Show him/her your goodness and truth
in everything he/she studies.
Keep his/her school and playground
free from violence.
We ask this through Christ our Lord. Amen.

3. Before Taking Tests

Lord,
you know the desires of our hearts.
Help _____ to do his/her best
on the tests he/she takes this day.
Help him/her remember what he/she has learned
and to answer the questions
completely and correctly.
Take away his/her fears
and give him/her trust in your care for him/her.
We ask this through Christ our Lord. Amen.

4. Returning from School

Lord,
we thank you for the study and learning
that have filled this day.
Keep us safe as we return home
and bless our evening hours
with the gift of your peace.
We ask this through Christ our Lord. Amen.

5. Going to a Religious Education Class

We praise you, God our Father,
for sending Jesus to be our brother
and to save us in your love.
Bless _____ and all the students
who will learn more about their faith
this (morning) (afternoon) (evening).
Fill their teachers with your wisdom
and with the power of your Gospel.
Send your Holy Spirit to help the students
know, love, and serve you.
Let what they learn
show them how to live
as followers of Jesus.
We ask this through Christ our Lord. Amen.

6. Taking a Child to Boarding School or College

Caring God,
we thank you for helping _____
to grow in wisdom and age.
Keep us safe as we take him/her to school
for a new year of learning.
Protect _____ from all fear and danger
during the coming weeks and months.
Give him/her the joy of good friends,
good classes,
and good health.
We ask this through Christ our Lord. Amen.

7. Visiting a Child at a Boarding School or College

Caring God,
we thank you for your gifts
that help _____
to grow in body, mind, and spirit.
Keep us safe
as we go to visit him/her at school.
Give your blessing to _____,
to his/her friends and teachers,
and to all whom we meet.
Let us enjoy our time together
and bring us home safely.
We ask this through Christ our Lord. Amen.

8. Going to Graduation Exercises or Party

Praise and thanks to you,
Heavenly Father,
for bringing _____
to the day of his/her graduation.
Look on him/her with love
as he/she leaves school
and prepares for new tasks in new places.
Help him/her to use his/her many skills
for your glory and for the good of others.
Be with us
as we travel to this glad celebration,
and bring us home safely.
We ask this through Christ our Lord. Amen.

9. Bringing a Newborn Infant Home from the Hospital

Heavenly Father,
when Jesus, your only Son,
was born into our world,
the angels sang for joy.
Today we thank you and praise you
for giving us _____
to be part of our family.
As we go to bring him/her and his/her mother
home from the hospital,
we ask your blessing upon us.
Make us a holy family,
and keep us safe in your love.
We ask this through Christ our Lord. Amen.

10. Eating a Meal in the Car

God of comings and goings,
during our busy days
your care for us never ends.
Bless the food
we are about to eat on our laps,
and help us keep it there.
Let it nourish us and strengthen us
for all that we have yet to do,
and let it remind us of your merciful love
in all our needs.
We ask this through Christ our Lord. Amen.

11. Going on an Adventure

God of surprises,
now we set out to explore a place
we have never been to,
to meet new people,
and to find new signs
of your wonderful love.
Protect us in all we say and do,
so that we may enjoy
what is tried-and-true
and what is new.
We ask this through Christ our Lord. Amen.

12. Going Fishing

Holy God, maker of the world,
praise be yours for swimming things!
You have given us many lakes and rivers
and the fish they contain.
Bless us on this fishing trip.
Protect us from the dangers of wind and rain
and from every accident,
and give us a bountiful catch.
May Jesus, who calmed the storm,
bring us all safely
to the shore of light and peace.
We ask this through Christ our Lord. Amen.

13. Going Hunting

How wonderful are your works, O Lord!
Cattle and sheep,
wild beasts of the field,
birds of the sky:
All of them tell your greatness.
Bless us on this hunting trip.
Keep us safe from all harm
and protect us from every accident.
Let carefulness and sportsmanship be ours
in what we say and do.
We ask this through Christ our Lord. Amen.

14. Going to Practice

God of work and play,
you give us strength
for body, soul, and spirit.
Be with us as we set out for practice.
Show _____ what he/she is to do,
and help him/her to do it well.
Let teamwork and respect for others
fill the words and deeds of everyone,
so that this practice will help them
to do their best.
We ask this through Christ our Lord. Amen.

15. Going to a Game, Meet, or Tournament

God of work and play,
you give us strength
for body, soul, and spirit.
Help _____ and his/her teammates
to do their best
during this (game) (meet) (tournament).
Keep all the players safe from injury.
Show them, their coaches and officials,
and their fans
how to respect each other
in all they say and do.
Let fair play and sportsmanship
guide the actions of everyone,
so that we can enjoy this time together.
We ask this through Christ our Lord. Amen.

16. Going Shopping

Lord,
all that we need comes from your hand.
As we set out on this shopping trip,
we ask you to watch over us.
The stores that we enter
are full of many signs of your care
for body and spirit.
Help us to choose wisely
from among all the things
that we find there,
and show us how to use them well.
Never let us forget
those who lack food to eat
and clothes to wear.
Give to all people
the good things that make life enjoyable.
Protect us as we make our way
from store to store
and as we return home.
We ask this through Christ our Lord. Amen.

17. Going on a Sleep-over

Lord of all times and places,
you are close to us, wherever we are.
Bless _____
as he/she prepares to spend this night
at the home of his/her friend _____.
Keep them safe from harm,
so that this time may be filled with joy.
Send your holy angels to keep them in peace
and to protect them while they sleep.
We ask this through Christ our Lord. Amen.

18. Going to Sunday Eucharist or Sunday Worship

Praise be yours, Lord, on this Sunday,
the day that you have made your own.
Thank you for calling your people together
each week to worship you.
Bless us on our way to church.
Be powerfully present
in every word we speak and hear,
in every note we sing,
and in every action we perform.
In all we say and do,
may yours be the praise and the glory.
We ask this through Christ our Lord. Amen.

19. Going Trick-or-Treating on Halloween

Praise to you, saving God,
for the holy men, women, and children
who live with you in the glory of heaven.
On this eve of All Saints Day,
send your blessing on _____
and on all trick-or-treaters,
and keep them safe this night.
Grant that all children
who suffer from abuse and violence
may find help and protection
in their need.
For them and for _____,
let your love be sweeter to their taste
than Halloween candy in their mouths.
We ask this through Christ our Lord. Amen.

20. Going on Vacation

Lord, in our work and play
we know your goodness and love.
Bless us with joy
as we set out for our days of vacation.
Let them bring us rest and refreshment.
Protect us as we travel.
Give us gentle weather and peaceful times.
Be with us at the meals we enjoy
and in the activities we share.
In all we do,
let us grow in our love for you
and for each other.
We ask this through Christ our Lord. Amen.

21. Going to Work

Lord, by our human labor
you renew and complete your creation.
Send your blessing upon us
as we leave for work.
Open our minds and hands
to do our tasks well.
Help us build up your kingdom
through what we do this day,
and keep us safe from all harm.
We ask this through Christ our Lord. Amen.

22. Learning to Drive a Car

Lord, you are with us
on our journey through life.
As _____ learns to drive,
we ask your guidance
in what we say and do.
Let carefulness and patience be ours
during this time of learning
and in all our driving.
Keep us safe in your love.
We ask this through Christ our Lord. Amen.

23. Stopping to Marvel at God's Creation

Praise to you, Lord, for the great love
which brought our world to birth!
You have filled this place
with your beauty and glory.
As we thank you for the wonders of nature,
deepen our respect for your creation
and let us share your joy
in all that you have made.
We ask this through Christ our Lord. Amen.

24. Taking a Child to a Date

Ever-faithful God,
where charity and love are found,
you are there.
We know your great love for us
in our family and friends.
Bless _____ as he/she sets out
to enjoy this time with his/her friend _____.
Let them find your goodness and kindness
in each other,
and guard them from all harm.
We ask this through Christ our Lord. Amen.

25. Visiting Friends

Lord God,
the friends of Jesus happily welcomed him
to their home.
We thank you for our friends _____ and _____,
who have invited us to visit them.
Keep us safe as we travel,
and fill our time together
with your joy and goodness.
We ask this through Christ our Lord. Amen.

GOING PLACES

26. Going to an Amusement Park

Lord,
you lift our spirits
higher than a roller coaster.
Your love is sweeter to our taste
than cotton candy.
Protect us as we set out
for a day of fun and games.
Keep us safe on the rides
and in all we do.
After this happy time together,
bring us home safely.
We ask this through Christ our Lord. Amen.

27. Going to a Birthday Party

Lord Jesus, our brother,
you were born into a human family,
just as we are.
As we travel to _____'s birthday party,
bless him/her
and all who will celebrate with him/her
on this happy day.
Help him/her to grow in wisdom and age and grace
before you and in the sight of all.
May your gift of love
be _____'s lasting joy,
now and always.
We ask this through Christ our Lord. Amen.

28. Going to the Cabin

Lord, in your goodness
you have given us a cabin in the woods,
a special place to share as a family.
Guard us on our way there
and during our days there.
Keep us safe
as we enjoy the wonders of land and water.
We ask this through Christ our Lord. Amen.

29. Returning from the Cabin

Lord,
we thank you for the time
we have spent at our cabin.
As we return home,
give us your protection.
Let your love carry us along the miles
quickly and safely.
We ask this through Christ our Lord. Amen.

30. Going to a Concert or Recital

In the sight of the angels,
we sing your praises, Lord.
Joining their chorus,
we thank you for the voices we raise in song,
for the ability to play musical instruments,
and for all our musical talents.
Be with us as we travel to _____'s (concert) (recital).
Open our ears and hearts
to enjoy your gift of music.
We ask this through Christ our Lord. Amen.

31. Going to the Doctor or Dentist

Lord Jesus, you care for us
in body and spirit.
Be with us as we take _____
to see the (doctor) (dentist).
Take away his/her fear
and bless him/her with good health.
Let your great love surround him/her,
this day and every day to come.
We ask this through Christ our Lord. Amen.

32. Going to the Emergency Room

Heavenly Father,
your Son, Jesus, brought your saving power
to those in need.
Hear our prayer for _____,
who needs your help right now.
As we take him/her to the emergency room,
let us find there
many signs of your care for us.
Take away our fears
and give us trust in your love.
We ask this through Christ our Lord. Amen.

33. Going to the Movies

Lord of sights and sounds,
protect us as we set out for the movies.
They take us to times and places
that we have not lived in
and cannot get to,
and they let us share the lives
of many different people.
Let what we see and hear at the movies
be for our good, not our harm.
May the movie we see
show us what is good and true and beautiful,
so that we may love it and live by it.
We ask this through Christ our Lord. Amen.

34. Going to a Play

Lord of sights and sounds,
through plays and drama
stories come to life before our eyes.
Protect us as we set out for _____'s play.
Be with him/her
and with all the cast and crew,
and help them to do their best
during this performance.
Let everyone enjoy this time together.
We ask this through Christ our Lord. Amen.

35. Going out to Eat

Nourishing God,
many are the kinds of food
that come to us in your goodness.
As we go out to eat,
we thank you for giving us this time
to enjoy them as a family.
Bless those who will prepare our food
and those who will serve it to us.
May our meal draw us closer to you
and to each other
in lasting love and peace.
We ask this through Christ our Lord. Amen.

36. Going to a Picnic or Barbeque

Lord,
you give food to all living things.
Be with us today
as we set out to enjoy a (picnic) (barbeque).
Bless us and the food we will share
in your good and beautiful world.
Protect us from all harm
and bring us back safely to our home.
We ask this through Christ our Lord. Amen.

37. Going to Summer Camp

God of heaven and earth,
praise be yours for the wonderful world
that you have made for us.
Bless _____
as he/she enjoys your creation
during his/her days at camp.
Show him/her your love
in good friends,
new experiences,
gentle weather,
and the beauty of nature.
Protect the campers
from all harm and danger
by day and night,
and bring them home safely.
We ask this through Christ our Lord. Amen.

38. Going to the Zoo or Animal Park

Lord, maker of all that lives,
we praise you for giving us delight
in the wonderful animals
that share our world.
Protect us as we go to see them
at the (zoo) (animal park).
Help us and all people
to be kind to animals.
Deepen our love for all your creatures.
We ask this through Christ our Lord. Amen.

39. Taking a Sick or Injured Pet to the Veterinarian or Animal Hospital

Heavenly Father,
we thank you for giving us _____
to be our pet.
Look with kindness on him/her
as we go to the (veterinarian) (animal hospital).
Restore him/her to full health and strength,
so that we may find delight
in this pet that you have made.
We ask this through Christ our Lord. Amen.

40. Going to a Family Gathering or Reunion

God of love, we give you praise and glory.
Thank you for making us a family,
brothers and sisters of Jesus Christ.
Be with us in times of joy and sorrow,
and help us in all our needs.
Protect us now
as we travel to our family (gathering) (reunion).
Let our celebration
give us the happiness that Jesus knew
in the company of his family and friends.
We ask this through Christ our Lord. Amen.

41. Taking a Child to Visit a Divorced Parent

Lord, you care for us
as parents care for their children.
Be with us as we take_____
to visit his/her (mom) (dad).
Let them enjoy their time together
in peace and safety.
We ask this through Christ our Lord. Amen.

42. Visiting a Child or Parent in the Hospital

Heavenly Father,
your Son, Jesus, showed special love
for the sick.
Listen as we call out to you in his name.
Be with us as we visit _____.
Bring him/her back to health,
comfort him/her with your peace,
and strengthen him/her in body and spirit.
Guide the doctors and nurses
who are caring for _____,
so that they will know what to do
and do it well.
Take away our fears
and give us trust in your power to save.
We ask this through Christ our Lord. Amen.

43. Visiting a Sick Relative or Friend at Home

Heavenly Father,
your Son, Jesus, showed special love
for the sick,
and brought your saving power
to their homes.
Be with us as we visit _____.
Bring him/her back to health,
comfort him/her with your peace,
and strengthen him/her in body and spirit.
We ask this through Christ our Lord. Amen.

44. Visiting Grandparents

Lord God, we praise you for giving us Jesus,
the son of the Blessed Virgin Mary
and grandson of Saints Joachim and Anne.
Look upon us with love
as we travel to visit _____ and _____,
our grandparents.
Keep us all safe and healthy.
Fill the time that we spend together
with your blessings of happiness and peace.
We ask this through Christ our Lord. Amen.

CELEBRATING SPECIAL RELIGIOUS OCCASIONS

45. Baptism

We give you thanks and praise,
Father of our Lord Jesus Christ.
Today we bring _____
to church for baptism.
Through water and the Holy Spirit,
he/she will become your beloved child.
Show him/her how to follow Jesus, our brother,
as he/she grows up and grows older.
Bless his/her godparents, _____ and _____,
as they help _____
die to sin and live for Jesus.
Through the prayers of _____'s patron saints,
bring him/her and all of us
to your heavenly kingdom.
We ask this through Christ our Lord. Amen.

46. First Holy Communion or Confirmation

Heavenly Father,
from the day of our baptism
you guide us as we follow your Son,
Jesus Christ.
Bless your son/daughter _____
as we prepare to celebrate
his/her (first holy communion) (confirmation).
Give him/her the grace
to live in faith, hope, and love,
and help our family
to come closer to you this day.
We ask this through Christ our Lord. Amen.

47. Wake or Funeral

Holy God,
all life comes from you
and to you it shall return.
Have mercy on _____
who has died in Christ but lives with you.
As we travel to _____'s (wake) (funeral),
hear our prayer.
Lead him/her and all who have died
to the unending joys of your kingdom.
In this time of sorrow,
let us and _____'s family
know your love and peace.
We ask this through Christ our Lord. Amen.

48. Wedding

Heavenly Father,
we praise you for the love
which unites _____ and _____
in marriage this day.
Protect us and all who travel to their wedding.
Make it a time of glad celebration
and fill this day with great happiness.
Give your many blessings
to _____ and _____,
to their families and friends,
and to their guests,
now and always.
We ask this through Christ our Lord. Amen.

49. Wedding Anniversary

We praise you, maker of man and woman,
for the love that _____ and _____ have shared
throughout (number) years of marriage.
We ask your blessing upon them,
[their children,] their relatives, and friends.
Protect all who travel to celebrate this anniversary,
and let us share the joy of heaven,
today and always.
We ask this through Christ our Lord. Amen.

50. Ordination

All-caring God,
you continue the saving work of your Son
through the work of your ministers.
Bless us as we travel to _____ 's ordination.
Strengthen him/her to give his/her life
in generous service to you and your church
as a (priest) (deacon) (minister).
Let him/her become more like Christ,
the Good Shepherd,
in all that he/she says and does.
After the celebration of this happy day,
let us and all _____ 's guests
return home safely,
praising your goodness to him/her
and to your holy people.
We ask this through Christ our Lord. Amen.

FACING TROUBLE ON THE ROAD

51. Car Trouble

Lord,
you are close to us in every need.
Our car is stopped right here,
but your love for us never stops.
Please give us your help!
Keep us calm and safe.
Show us what we need to do,
so that soon
we may be on our way again,
thankful that you are with us.
We ask this through Christ our Lord. Amen.

52. During a Storm

Lord,
amid pouring rain,
crashing thunder,
and flashing lightning,
we ask you to help us!
Surround us with your power
as with a shield.
Let no harm come to us
during this storm,
but give us trust
in your care for us.
Send your Holy Spirit
to take away our fears
and calm our hearts.
We ask this through Christ our Lord. Amen.

or:

Lord,
amid blowing snow
and howling winds,
we ask you to help us!
Surround us with your power
as with a shield.
Let no harm come to us
during this storm,
but give us trust
in your care for us.
Send your Holy Spirit
to take away our fears
and calm our hearts.
We ask this through Christ our Lord. Amen.

53. Looking for a Parking Place

Loving God,
we always have a place in your heart,
but now we can't find a place
to park our car.
Please give us what we need,
and keep us safe wherever we go.
We ask this through Christ our Lord. Amen.

54. Stuck in a Traffic Jam

Lord,
lots of traffic has brought us to a stop,
but your love for us never stops.
As we wait here,
make us respectful and patient.
Let your peace fill our hearts,
now and always,
and send us on our way in good time.
We ask this through Christ our Lord. Amen.

55. Waiting at a Stop Light

On red:

Leader or All: On red we stop and wait,
No matter if we're late.

All: Lord, keep us safe this day.
Lord, hear us as we pray:
Have mercy, Lord, have mercy.

On green:

Leader or All: On green we move ahead,
God's angel not outsped.

All: Lord, keep us safe this day.
Lord, hear us as we pray:
Have mercy, Lord, have mercy.

56. Waiting for a Train to Pass

Leader or All: Right here we stop and wait,
a train has closed the gate.

All: Lord, keep us safe this day.
Lord, hear us as we pray:
Have mercy, Lord, have mercy.

(This section of the prayer may be repeated during the wait:)

Leader or all: We wait and wait some more.
This waiting's such a bore!

All: Lord, keep us safe this day.
Lord, hear us as we pray:
Have mercy, Lord, have mercy.

Leader or All: It's time to move ahead!
The train so fast has sped!

All: Lord, keep us safe this day.
Lord, hear us as we pray:
Have mercy, Lord, have mercy.

57. When Lost

Lord of north and south, east and west,
you are always ready
to help those who have lost their way.
Hear our prayer!
Show us the way to where we want to go,
and bring us there quickly and safely.
We ask this through Christ our Lord. Amen.

58. When Seeing an Ambulance Go By or Passing the Site of an Accident

Lord,
a speeding ambulance tells us
that someone is injured and in pain,
and needs your saving help right now.
Be with all who are hurt in this accident.
Ease their suffering
and make them whole again
in your merciful love.
Guide the minds and hands
of those who care for them,
so that a full and speedy recovery
may be theirs.
We ask this through Christ our Lord. Amen.

PRAYERS FOR TRAVELING

VARIOUS TRAVEL PRAYERS

1. All-powerful and merciful God,
   you led the children of Israel on dry land,
   parting the waters of the sea;
   you guided the Magi to your Son by a star.
   So great was your love for us
   that you gave us Jesus
   to be our way to you.
   Watch over us as we travel.
   Bless us with your protection
   and accompany us on our journey.
   Help us to travel in peace and safety
   until we return.
   We ask this grace through Christ our Lord. Amen.

2. O God, you called your servant, Abraham,
   and kept him from evil on his journey.
   We ask you to keep us under your care.
   Be to us, O Lord,
   a comfort on the way,
   a shadow from the heat,
   a shelter from the rain and cold,
   a refuge in trouble.
   Lead us,
   that we may safely arrive at our destination
   and happily return to our home.
   We ask this through Christ our Lord. Amen.

3. All-powerful God,
   bless us with every heavenly blessing
   and give us a safe journey.
   Wherever life leads us,
   may we find you there to protect us.
   We ask this through Christ our Lord. Amen.

4. Almighty God,
   bless us and hear our prayers for a safe journey. Amen.

5. Lord God,
   guide us in paths of peace.
   Send your holy angel Raphael
   to accompany us on our way,
   so that we may return home safe and sound,
   in peace and joy.
   We ask this through Christ our Lord. Amen.

6. Lord God,
   you sent your holy archangel Raphael
   to be the fellow-traveler of the young Tobias.
   Grant that this powerful bringer of healing
   may always shield, help, and defend us.
   We ask this through Christ our Lord. Amen.

7. Raphael with Tobias:
   Gabriel with Mary:
   Michael with the heavenly host:
   be our companions along the way. Amen.

8. Almighty God,
   through your Holy Spirit
   you strengthen our faith,
   the faith which Saint Christopher professed
   by shedding his blood.
   As we set out on this journey,
   free us from every danger
   by his powerful prayers.
   We ask this through Christ our Lord. Amen.

TRAVEL PRAYER IN THE MORNING

All make the sign of the cross.

Leader: Everlasting is the love of our God,

All: the Father, the Son, ✠ and the Holy Spirit. Amen.

or:

Leader: Rich in kindness is our God,

All: the Father, the Son, ✠ and the Holy Spirit. Amen.

One of these psalms is prayed:

A) Psalm 25:4–5abc,6 and 7cd,8–9

Solo: Remember your mercy, O Lord.

All: Remember your mercy, O Lord.

Solo: Show me your paths
and teach me to follow;
guide me by your truth
and instruct me.
You keep me safe.

All: Remember your mercy, O Lord.

Solo: Please, Lord, remember,
you have always
been patient and kind.
Show how truly kind you are
and remember me.

All: Remember your mercy, O Lord.

Solo: You are honest and merciful
and you teach sinners
how to follow your path.
You lead humble people
to do what is right
and to stay on your path.

All: Remember your mercy, O Lord.

All: Glory to the Father, and to the Son,
and to the Holy Spirit:
as it was in the beginning, is now,
and will be for ever. Amen.

or:

B) Psalm 34:1–2,7–8,17–18

Solo: Glory and praise to you, Lord!

All: Glory and praise to you, Lord!

Solo: I will always praise the Lord.
With all my heart,
I will praise the Lord.
Let all who are helpless
listen and be glad.

All: Glory and praise to you, Lord!

Solo: If you honor the Lord,
his angel will protect you.
Discover for yourself
that the Lord is kind.
Come to him for protection,
and you will be glad.

All: Glory and praise to you, Lord!

Solo: When his people pray for help,
he listens and rescues them
from their troubles.
The Lord is there to rescue
all who are discouraged
and have given up hope.

All: Glory and praise to you, Lord!

All: Glory to the Father, and to the Son,
and to the Holy Spirit:
as it was in the beginning, is now,
and will be for ever. Amen.

or:

C) Psalm 90:12–13,14abc,17

Solo: Lord, help us in your love.

All: Lord, help us in your love.

Solo: Our Lord, teach us to use wisely
all the time we have.
Help us, Lord! Don't wait!
Pity your servants.

All: Lord, help us in your love.

Solo: When morning comes,
let your love satisfy
all our needs.
Our Lord and our God,
treat us with kindness
and let all go well for us.
Please let all go well!

All: Lord, help us in your love.

All: Glory to the Father, and to the Son,
and to the Holy Spirit:
as it was in the beginning, is now,
and will be for ever. Amen.

or:

D) Psalm 103:1–2,3–4,5,11

Solo: Bless the Lord, my soul!

All: Bless the Lord, my soul!

Solo: With all my heart
I praise the Lord,
and with all that I am
I praise his holy name!
With all my heart
I praise the Lord!
I will never forget
how kind he has been.

All: Bless the Lord, my soul!

Solo: The Lord forgives our sins,
heals us when we are sick,
and protects us from death.
His kindness and love
are a crown on our heads.

All: Bless the Lord, my soul!

Solo: Each day that we live,
he provides for our needs
and gives us the strength
of a young eagle.
How great is God's love for all
who worship him?
Greater than the distance
between heaven and earth!

All: Bless the Lord, my soul!

All: Glory to the Father, and to the Son,
and to the Holy Spirit:
as it was in the beginning, is now,
and will be for ever. Amen.

or:

E) Psalm 143:1,8,10

Solo: Lord, hear our prayer.

All: Lord, hear our prayer.

Solo: Listen, Lord, as I pray!
You are faithful and honest
and will answer my prayer.

All: Lord, hear our prayer.

Solo: Each morning let me learn
more about your love
because I trust you.
I come to you in prayer,
asking for your guidance.

All: Lord, hear our prayer.

Solo: You are my God.
Show me what you want me to do,
and let your gentle Spirit
lead me in the right path.

All: Lord, hear our prayer.

All: Glory to the Father, and to the Son,
and to the Holy Spirit:
as it was in the beginning, is now,
and will be for ever. Amen.

or:

F) Psalm 145:1–2,8–9,13cd–14

Solo: I will praise your name for ever.

All: I will praise your name for ever.

Solo: I will praise you,
my God and King,
and always honor your name.
I will praise you each day
and always honor your name.

All: I will praise your name for ever.

Solo: You are merciful, Lord!
You are kind and patient
and always loving.
You are good to everyone,
and you take care
of all your creation.

All: I will praise your name for ever.

Solo: Our Lord, you keep your word
and do everything you say.
When someone stumbles or falls,
you give a helping hand.

All: I will praise your name for ever.

All: Glory to the Father, and to the Son,
and to the Holy Spirit:
as it was in the beginning, is now,
and will be for ever. Amen.

Scripture Reading

Deuteronomy 6:4–7

A reading from the Book of Deuteronomy.

"Israel, remember this! The LORD—and the LORD alone—is our God. Love the LORD your God with all your heart, with all your soul, and with all your strength. Never forget these commands that I am giving you today. Teach them to your children. Repeat them when you are at home and when you are away, when you are resting and when you are working."

Reader: The word of the Lord.

All: Thanks be to God.

or:

Lamentations 3:22–25

A reading from the Book of Lamentations.

The LORD's unfailing love and mercy still continue,
fresh as the morning, as sure as the sunrise.

The LORD is all I have, and so in him I put my hope.
The LORD is good to everyone who trusts in him.

Reader: The word of the Lord.

All: Thanks be to God.

or:

Romans 8:26–27

A reading from the Letter of St. Paul to the Romans.

The Spirit also comes to help us, weak as we are. For we do not know how we ought to pray; the Spirit himself pleads with God for us in groans that words cannot express. And God, who sees into our hearts, knows what the thought of the Spirit is; because the Spirit pleads with God on behalf of his people and in accordance with his will.

Reader: The word of the Lord.

All: Thanks be to God.

Silent Reflection

Response to the Reading

Leader: Lord Jesus, be with us throughout this day:

All: In all we do and all we say.

or:

Leader: Lord, be our strength every morning,

All: Our help in time of need.

Intercessions (petitions) may be prayed.

Lord's Prayer

Leader: Let us place all our trust in God as we pray the Lord's Prayer:

All: Our Father ....

Prayer for the Occasion or Activity

See pages 3–33. *Prayed by the leader or by all.*

Blessing

Leader: May the Lord guard us from danger this day and strengthen us in the ways of peace, now and for ever.

All: Amen.

TRAVEL PRAYER AT NOONTIME

All make the sign of the cross.

Leader: Let us call upon our God,

All: the Father, the Son, ✠ and the Holy Spirit. Amen.

or:

Leader: God is close to us in every need,

All: the Father, the Son, ✠ and the Holy Spirit. Amen.

One of these psalms is prayed:

A) Psalm 71:1–2,3abcd,3ef,5a

Solo: I will sing of your salvation.

All: I will sing of your salvation.

Solo: I run to you, Lord,
for protection.
Don't disappoint me.
You do what is right,
so come to my rescue.
Listen to my prayer
and keep me safe.

All: I will sing of your salvation.

Solo: Be my mighty rock,
the place where I can always run
for protection
Save me by your command!

All: I will sing of your salvation.

Solo: You are my mighty rock
and my fortress.
I depend on you.

All: I will sing of your salvation.

All: Glory to the Father, and to the Son,
and to the Holy Spirit:
as it was in the beginning, is now,
and will be for ever. Amen.

or:

B) Psalm 121:1–2,5–6,7–8

Solo: Our help is from the Lord.

All: Our help is from the Lord.

Solo: I look to the hills!
Where will I find help?
It will come from the Lord,
who created the heavens
and the earth.

All: Our help is from the Lord.

Solo: The Lord is your protector,
there at your right side
to shade you from the sun.
You won't be harmed
by the sun during the day
or by the moon at night.

All: Our help is from the Lord.

Solo: The Lord will protect you
and keep you safe
from all dangers.
The Lord will protect you
now and always
wherever you are.

All: Our help is from the Lord.

All: Glory to the Father, and to the Son,
and to the Holy Spirit:
as it was in the beginning, is now,
and will be for ever. Amen.

or:

C) Psalm 146:6d–7ab,8b–9a

Solo: Praise the Lord!

All: Praise the Lord!

Solo: God always keeps his word.
He gives justice to the poor
and food to the hungry.

All: Praise the Lord!

Solo: The Lord gives a helping hand
to everyone who falls.
The Lord loves good people
and looks after strangers.

All: Praise the Lord!

All: Glory to the Father, and to the Son,
and to the Holy Spirit:
as it was in the beginning, is now,
and will be for ever. Amen.

Scripture Reading

Tobit 4:19

A reading from the Book of Tobit.

[Tobit said to his son Tobias:] “Take advantage of every opportunity to praise the Lord your God. Ask him to make you prosper in whatever you set out to do. He does not give his wisdom to the people of any other nation. He is the source of all good things.”

Reader: The word of the Lord.

All: Thanks be to God.

or:

Genesis 28:14b–15

A reading from the Book of Genesis.

[The Lord said to Jacob:] “Through you and your descendants I will bless all the nations. Remember, I will be with you and protect you wherever you go, and I will bring you back to this land. I will not leave you until I have done all that I have promised you.”

Reader: The word of the Lord.

All: Thanks be to God.

Silent Reflection

Response to the Reading

Leader: Lord, make me know your ways.

All: Lord, teach me your paths.

or:

Leader: Lord, we trust in your merciful love.

All: We rejoice in your saving help.

Intercessions (petitions) may be prayed.

Lord's Prayer

Leader: Let us pray the prayer that Jesus gave us:

All: Our Father ....

Prayer for the Occasion or Activity

See pages 3–33. Prayed by the leader or by all.

Blessing

Leader: May the cross of Jesus be to us a source of blessing and life, both now and for ever.

All: Amen.

TRAVEL PRAYER IN THE EVENING

All make the sign of the cross.

Leader: Holy and strong is our God, living for ever:

All: the Father, the Son, ✠ and the Holy Spirit. Amen.

or:

Leader: Evenings and mornings, bless the Lord!
Praise and glorify God for ever:

All: the Father, the Son, ✠ and the Holy Spirit. Amen.

One of these psalms is prayed:

A) Psalm 16:1–2a,5,7–8,11

Solo: Lord, show us the path of life.

All: Lord, show us the path of life.

Solo: Protect me, Lord God!
I run to you for safety,
and I have said,
"Only you are my Lord!"
You, Lord, are all I want!
You are my choice,
and you keep me safe.

All: Lord, show us the path of life.

Solo: I praise you, Lord,
for being my guide.
Even in the darkest night,
your teachings fill my mind.
I will always look to you,
as you stand beside me
and protect me from fear.

All: Lord, show us the path of life.

Solo: You have shown me
the path to life,
and you make me glad
by being near to me.
Sitting at your right side,
I will always be joyful.

All: Lord, show us the path of life.

All: Glory to the Father, and to the Son,
and to the Holy Spirit:
as it was in the beginning, is now,
and will be for ever. Amen.

or:

B) Psalm 23:1–3a,3b–4,6

Solo: The Lord is my shepherd;
there is nothing I shall want.

All: The Lord is my shepherd;
there is nothing I shall want.

Solo: You, Lord, are my shepherd.
I will never be in need.
You let me rest in fields
of green grass.
You lead me to streams
of peaceful water,
and you refresh my life.

All: The Lord is my shepherd;
there is nothing I shall want.

Solo: You are true to your name,
and you lead me
along the right paths.
I may walk through valleys
as dark as death,
but I won't be afraid.
You are with me,
and your shepherd's rod
makes me feel safe.

All: The Lord is my shepherd;
there is nothing I shall want.

Solo: Your kindness and love
will always be with me
each day of my life,
and I will live forever
in your house, Lord.

All: The Lord is my shepherd;
there is nothing I shall want.

All: Glory to the Father, and to the Son,
and to the Holy Spirit:
as it was in the beginning, is now,
and will be for ever. Amen.

or:

C) Psalm 27:1,7–8,13–14

Solo: The Lord is my light and my help.

All: The Lord is my light and my help.

Solo: You, Lord, are the light
that keeps me safe.
I am not afraid of anyone.
You protect me,
and I have no fears.

All: The Lord is my light and my help.

Solo: Please listen when I pray!
Have pity. Answer my prayer.
My heart tells me to pray.
I am eager to see your face.

All: The Lord is my light and my help.

Solo: I know that I will live
to see how kind you are.
Trust the Lord!
Be brave and strong
and trust the Lord.

All: The Lord is my light and my help.

All: Glory to the Father, and to the Son,
and to the Holy Spirit:
as it was in the beginning, is now,
and will be for ever. Amen.

or:

D) Psalm 31:1–2abcd–3,16,19

Solo: Lord, be my rock of safety.

All: Lord, be my rock of safety.

Solo: I come to you, Lord,
for protection.
Don't let me be ashamed.
Do as you have promised
and rescue me.
Listen to my prayer.

All: Lord, be my rock of safety.

Solo: Hurry to save me.
Be my mighty rock
and the fortress where I am safe.
Lead me and guide me,
so that your name
will be honored.
Smile on me, your servant.
Have pity and rescue me.

All: Lord, be my rock of safety.

Solo: You are wonderful,
and while everyone watches,
you store up blessings for all
who honor and trust you.

All: Lord, be my rock of safety.

All: Glory to the Father, and to the Son,
and to the Holy Spirit:
as it was in the beginning, is now,
and will be for ever. Amen.

or:

E) Psalm 69:13,16,29b–30a

Solo: Lord, in your great love, answer me.

All: Lord, in your great love, answer me.

Solo: I pray to you, Lord.
So when the time is right,
answer me and help me
with your wonderful love.

All: Lord, in your great love, answer me.

Solo: Answer me, Lord!
You are kind and good.
Pay attention to me!
You are truly merciful.

All: Lord, in your great love, answer me.

Solo: Protect me, God,
and keep me safe!
I will praise the Lord God
with a song.

All: Lord, in your great love, answer me.

All: Glory to the Father, and to the Son,
and to the Holy Spirit:
as it was in the beginning, is now,
and will be for ever. Amen.

or:

F) Psalm 85:8abc,9,10–11

Solo: Lord, show us your mercy and love.

All: Lord, show us your mercy and love.

Solo: I will listen to you, Lord God,
because you promise peace
to those who are faithful.
You are ready to rescue
everyone who worships you,
so that you will live with us
in all of your glory.

All: Lord, show us your mercy and love.

Solo: Love and loyalty
will come together;
goodness and peace will unite.
Loyalty will sprout
from the ground;
justice will look down
from the sky above.

All: Lord, show us your mercy and love.

All: Glory to the Father, and to the Son,
and to the Holy Spirit:
as it was in the beginning, is now,
and will be for ever. Amen.

Scripture Reading

Exodus 23:20–23a

A reading from the Book of Exodus.

[The Lord said to Moses:] "I will send an angel ahead of you to protect you as you travel and to bring you to the place which I have prepared. Pay attention to him and obey him. Do not rebel against him, for I have sent him, and he will not pardon such rebellion. But if you obey him and do everything I command, I will fight against all your enemies. My angel will go ahead of you."

Reader: The word of the Lord.

All: Thanks be to God.

or:

Sirach 2:10–11

A reading from the Book of Sirach.

Think back to the ancient generations and consider this: has the Lord ever disappointed anyone who put his hope in him? Has the Lord ever abandoned anyone who held him in constant reverence? Has the Lord ever ignored anyone who prayed to him? The Lord is kind and merciful; he forgives our sins and keeps us safe in time of trouble.

Reader: The word of the Lord.

All: Thanks be to God.

or:

Philippians 4:6–7

A reading from the Letter of St. Paul to the Philippians.

Don't worry about anything, but in all your prayers ask God for what you need, always asking him with a thankful heart. And God's peace, which is far beyond human understanding, will keep your hearts and minds safe in union with Christ Jesus.

Reader: The word of the Lord.

All: Thanks be to God.

Silent Reflection

Response to the Reading

Leader: O Lord, do not ever forsake me.

All: My God, be not far from me.

or:

Leader: Lord, my soul clings to you.

All: Your right hand holds me fast.

Intercessions (petitions) may be prayed.

Lord's Prayer

Leader: Remembering God's love and care for us, let us pray as Jesus taught us:

All: Our Father ....

Prayer for the Occasion or Activity

See pages 3–33. Prayed by the leader or by all.

Blessing

Leader: May God be with us in sorrow and in joy, and give us lasting light and peace, for ever and ever.

All: Amen.

TRAVEL PRAYER AT NIGHT

All make the sign of the cross.

Leader: God be with us as we end this day,

All: the Father, the Son, ✠ and the Holy Spirit. Amen.

or:

Leader: Darkness is not dark for our God,

All: the Father, the Son, ✠ and the Holy Spirit. Amen.

One of these psalms is prayed:

A) Psalm 4:1abef,3,6cd–7a

Solo: Lord, let your face shine on us.

All: Lord, let your face shine on us.

Solo: You are my God and protector.
Please answer my prayer.
Now have pity and listen as I pray.

All: Lord, let your face shine on us.

Solo: The Lord has chosen
everyone who is faithful
to be his very own,
and he answers my prayers.

All: Lord, let your face shine on us.

Solo: Let your kindness, Lord,
shine brightly on us.
You brought me happiness.

All: Lord, let your face shine on us.

All: Glory to the Father, and to the Son,
and to the Holy Spirit:
as it was in the beginning, is now,
and will be for ever. Amen.

or:

B) Psalm 91:1–2,9,11

Solo: In you, my God, I place my trust.

All: In you, my God, I place my trust.

Solo: Live under the protection
of God Most High
and stay in the shadow
of God All-Powerful.
Then you will say to the Lord,
"You are my fortress,
my place of safety;
you are my God,
and I trust you."

All: In you, my God, I place my trust.

Solo: The Lord Most High
is your fortress.
Run to him for safety.
God will command his angels
to protect you
wherever you go.

All: In you, my God, I place my trust.

All: Glory to the Father, and to the Son,
and to the Holy Spirit:
as it was in the beginning, is now,
and will be for ever. Amen.

Scripture Reading

Jeremiah 14:8a,9b

A reading from the Book of the prophet Jeremiah.

"[Lord,] you are Israel's only hope;
you are the one who saves us from disaster. ...
Surely, LORD, you are with us!
We are your people; do not abandon us."

Reader: The word of the Lord.

All: Thanks be to God.

or:

Ephesians 4:26,32

A reading from the Letter to the Ephesians.

If you become angry, do not let your anger lead you into sin, and do not stay angry all day. Don't give the Devil a chance. ... Instead, be kind and tender-hearted to one another, and forgive one another, as God has forgiven you through Christ.

Reader: The word of the Lord.

All: Thanks be to God.

Silent Reflection

Response to the Reading

Leader: Lord, you guard us like a shield.

All: No evil shall we fear.

or:

Leader: Lord, you are good and forgiving.

All: Full of love to all who call.

One of the travel prayers on pages 36–37 may be prayed by the leader or by all.

Blessing

Leader: May the peace of Christ remain with us this night and always, for ever and ever.

All: Amen.